Little Pieces of Poetry

Little Pieces of Poetry

Selected Poems 1998 - 2019

Garrett Buhl Robinson

Poetry, illustrations and book design created
by Garrett Buhl Robinson.

Garrett Buhl Robinson © 2020
All Rights Reserved

Poet in the Park™
In Humanity I see Grace, Beauty and Dignity.

PoetinthePark.com

Table of Contents

For Mom	1
A Sonnet for the Sonnet	2
Lit Figs	3
What It Is Is Its Worth	4
Singing for a Living	5
Brooklyn's Curious Birds	6
About Books	7
Hopeless Poem	8
A Momentous Notice	9
Voyager	10
Not a Poem	11
This May	12
One Is Always Odd	13
Pas Seul	14
Serenade	15
Mark Question	16
All Essential	17
Creative Nature	18
For Marianne Moore	19
Intimate with the Ancients	20
Hazel Hall	21
Ensemble of the Audience	22
Jester	23
For Ms. Bee	24
Love	25
Maps Are Metaphors	26
Proof of Life	27
Made of Strays	28
Troubadour	29
For a Romantic	30

Life — is what we make it —

                Emily Dickinson

For Mom

Once, I saw my Mom's hands still years ago,
perhaps the only time I've seen them rest
except at supper when our meals were blessed.
I've never seen the work of those hands slow,
spinning family flax into loving gold
and when she saw where my eyes had set
she confessed with modest self-consciousness,
"Isn't it awful the way the veins show?"

Mom, your hands are of a most gracious beauty.
Those veins are swollen from devoted work.
The wise guidance of those hands have raised me.
When I misbehaved, they would make me smart.
The gentle care of those hands carried me
and will always hold me up to your heart.

                Garrett Buhl Robinson

A Sonnet for the Sonnet

Being a sonneteer, I am enamored
by sonnets, but today to my delight
serendipity favored me to find
a university class that explored
the passionate history of the form.
The lecture described this frame tumbling through lives,
uniting affections through centuries of time.
There is no language that it scorns,
there is no culture it cannot adorn.
This delicate and vigorous design
turns eternal in awakening minds
and endures with the desires it records.
I swear with my life and the lute I strum,
as long as we love sonnets will be sung.

              Garrett Buhl Robinson

Lit Figs

A poem cannot build you an abode
but it may help to make you feel at home.

A poem cannot provide sustenance
but strengthens with inspired encouragement.

A poem cannot quench your thirst
but the fluency may refresh with verse.

A poem cannot turn on the lights
but a passage may open new insights.

A poem cannot heal the sick
but may comfort you through convalescence.

A poem cannot not teach you math
but may provide lines into the abstract.

This poem isn't worth any money.
It circulates and appreciates beauty.

Garrett Buhl Robinson

What It Is Is Its Worth

I have been wandering off my whole life,
composing my own literary line
with the plodding steps of my curious mind.
I sing exalted songs while I rise
then lament each darkening decline.
I have endured the switchbacks while I climbed
lifted my arms into the empty sky
before I tumbled down the other side.
Then I stand back up time after time.
Perhaps it is all there is worthwhile,
perhaps it's all I ever wanted in life,
but there is a brutal beauty I cannot deny,
the wandering wonder where I abide,
I will always explore till I expire.

Garrett Buhl Robinson

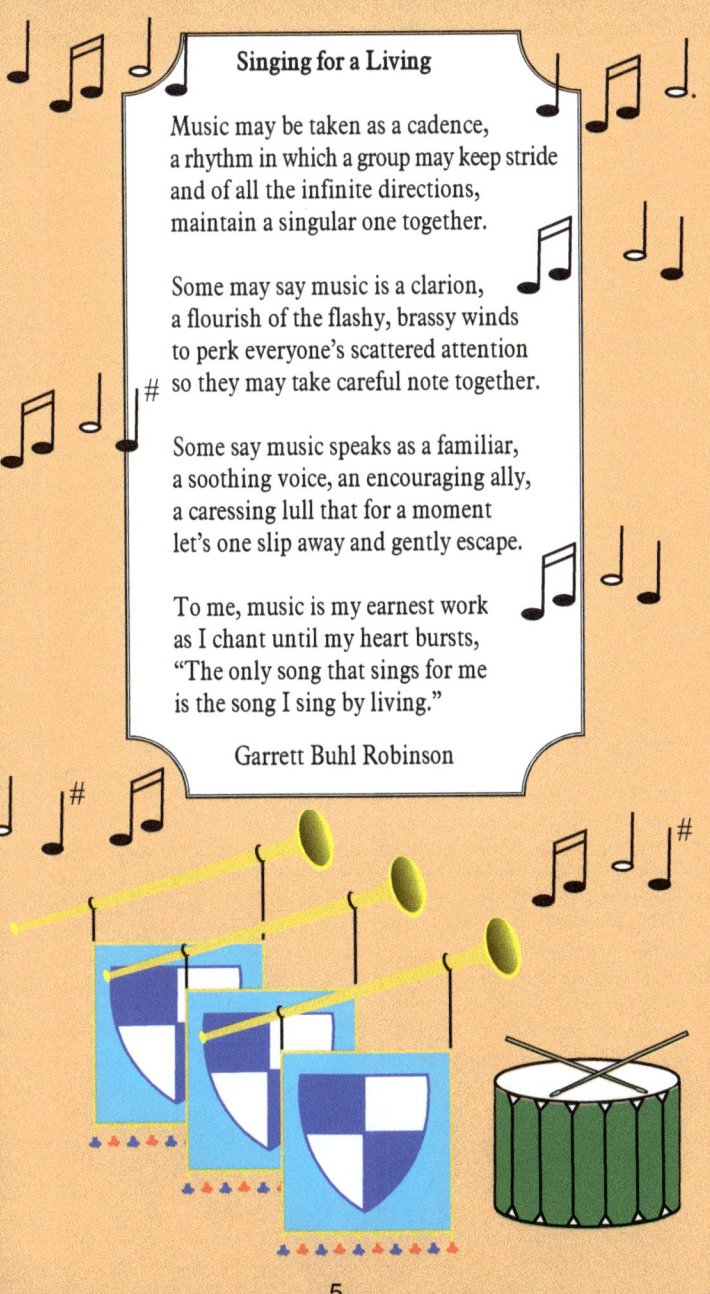

Singing for a Living

Music may be taken as a cadence,
a rhythm in which a group may keep stride
and of all the infinite directions,
maintain a singular one together.

Some may say music is a clarion,
a flourish of the flashy, brassy winds
to perk everyone's scattered attention
so they may take careful note together.

Some say music speaks as a familiar,
a soothing voice, an encouraging ally,
a caressing lull that for a moment
let's one slip away and gently escape.

To me, music is my earnest work
as I chant until my heart bursts,
"The only song that sings for me
is the song I sing by living."

Garrett Buhl Robinson

Brooklyn's Curious Birds

Immersed in my verse today, on a whim
I lifted my eyes and noted some birds
cocking their heads while observing me work
from perches at my window. I watch them often.
They live on the breeze cupped in their wings
arching between Brooklyn's buildings and trees
to coronate the urban canopy
when they pause to weave their nests and sing.
Some may say I live a similar way
riding the wind of my sequence of songs
in flight on wings of tuneful plumes,
yet I suspect that the birds are amazed
that I can scratch away the entire day
and find so much to peck on a blank page.

Garrett Buhl Robinson

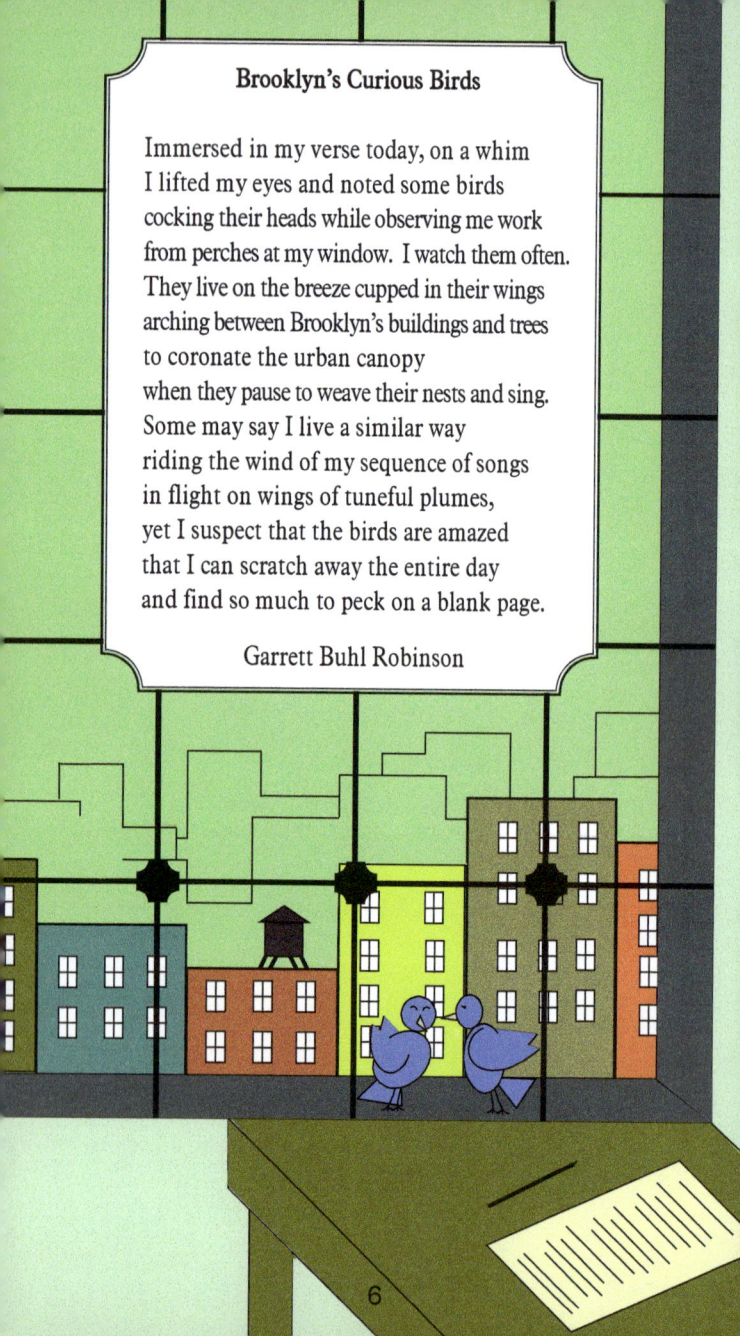

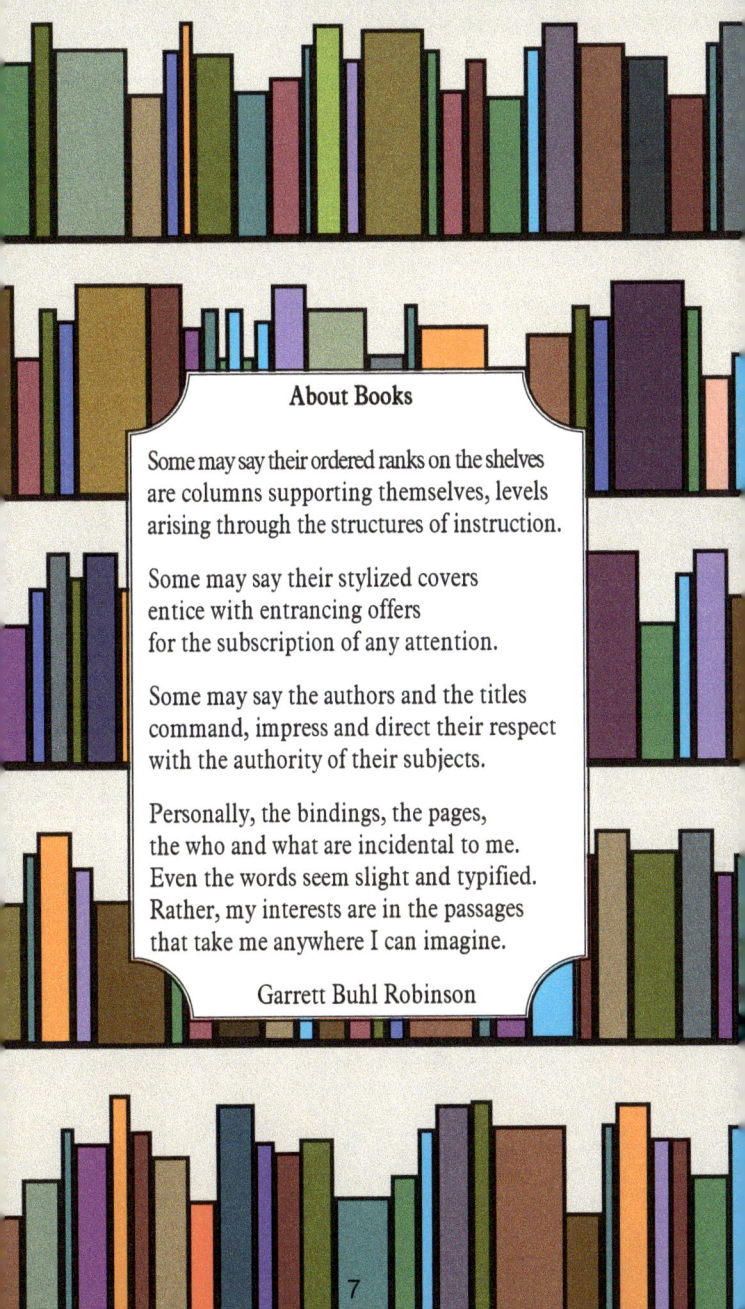

About Books

Some may say their ordered ranks on the shelves
are columns supporting themselves, levels
arising through the structures of instruction.

Some may say their stylized covers
entice with entrancing offers
for the subscription of any attention.

Some may say the authors and the titles
command, impress and direct their respect
with the authority of their subjects.

Personally, the bindings, the pages,
the who and what are incidental to me.
Even the words seem slight and typified.
Rather, my interests are in the passages
that take me anywhere I can imagine.

Garrett Buhl Robinson

Hopeless Poem

Sometimes I wonder if I am only
capable of making mistakes.
I always have the most uncanny
way to find precisely how anything breaks.
I've stepped off ledges while reaching for stars.
My bumbling always crumbles into jumbles.
I spend hours tuning stringless guitars
while boasting of times when I was humble.
I'll find something odd from the peas in a pod,
make a mess with nothing but emptiness.
Yet at least I know the roads I have trod
while I sing songs consoling the hopeless.
In the world's endless possibility,
failure is my failsafe consistency.

              Garrett Buhl Robinson

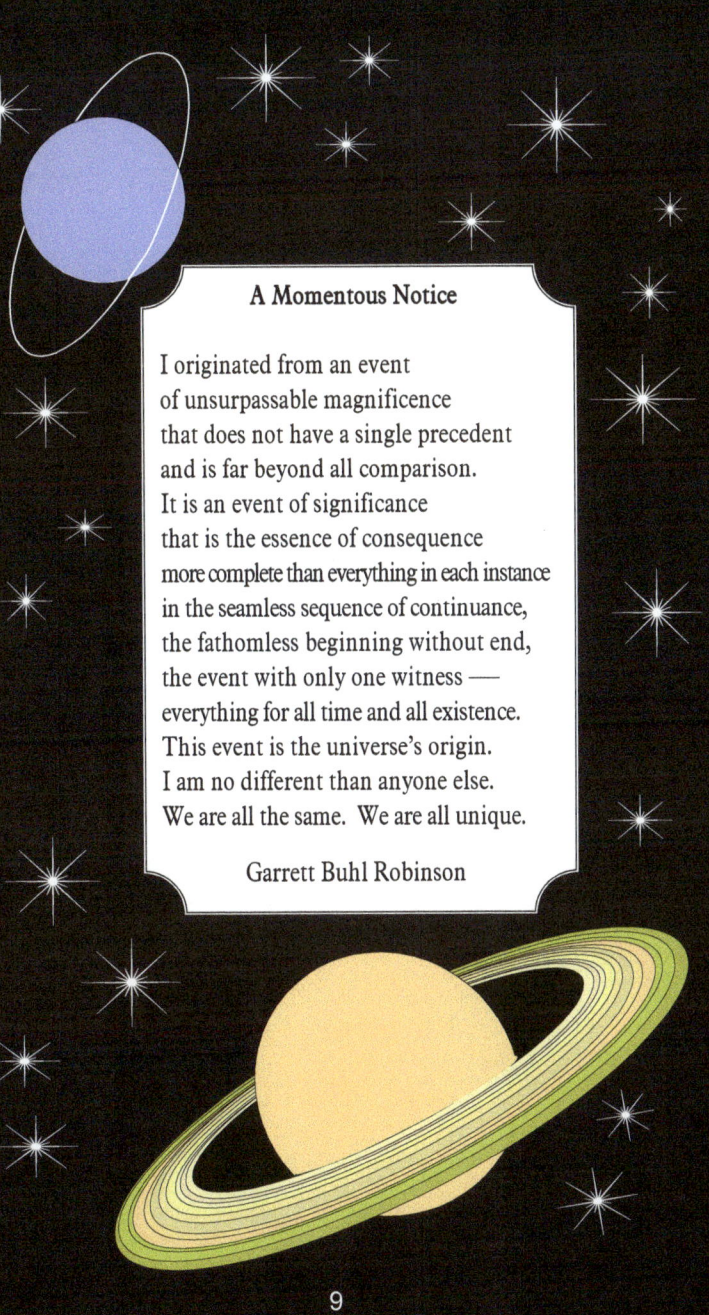

A Momentous Notice

I originated from an event
of unsurpassable magnificence
that does not have a single precedent
and is far beyond all comparison.
It is an event of significance
that is the essence of consequence
more complete than everything in each instance
in the seamless sequence of continuance,
the fathomless beginning without end,
the event with only one witness —
everything for all time and all existence.
This event is the universe's origin.
I am no different than anyone else.
We are all the same. We are all unique.

             Garrett Buhl Robinson

Voyager

With shelves of books and with the shelves themselves
I ribbed and sealed my hull and decked my craft.
Wonder is my prow, focus is my helm
and honest songs swell the sails of my masts
I made from my dock's straight and sturdy posts.
I know I won't need the dock anymore –
I can't commit myself into the open
if I try to keep one foot on the shore.
I am unmoored, I have found my release
into the ocean of eternity
with the schools of stars swimming through the deep
as I steer into the immensity.
I have become the ship, the sea, the wind
and I may never touch the land again.

Garrett Buhl Robinson

Not a Poem

This is not a poem.
This is a musical score allowing
you to play the most magnificent
instrument - your own mind.

This is not a poem.
This is a path you may travel
to mountains and fountains
of discovery within yourself.

This is not a poem.
This is a tool that touches
and the emotion evoked,
both spectacles and spectacle.

This is definitely not a poem.
This is anything you can imagine.

Garrett Buhl Robinson

This May

May your thoughts flourish with verse
and flutter with effortless ease
like the birds and butterflies
in the fragrant blooms of spring.

May your troubles calm
like a pond at dawn,
a mirror framed at the shore
where the willows' limber stems
bend to touch their reflection.

May the swans glide into the open
to rear in trumpeting majesty
then shake the mist from their wings
and running on their striding feet
leap into flight over uplifting trees.

Garrett Buhl Robinson

One Is Always Odd

Many have said the world is relative
but every moment is exactly what it is
and there is a perfect continuity
transforming through all that exists.
Some places may seem exotic to some
but then are commonplace to another
but the opinions and tastes of one person
do not define the being of the other.
Most often I am an anomaly,
a melody wandering through the fog.
I am a song and I am a singing
in the music playing my whole life long.
Really, it is self-explanatory:
The individual is always odd.

Garrett Buhl Robinson

Pas Seul

Clumsily we depict grace as a gift
that nature has flippantly bestowed
upon them but down the arduous road,
enclosed by the recital curtain's rift,
exhausting strains to lithe the tensing stiff
bodies aching with laborious loads
refresh the streams where elegance flows
and spring to life ballet's delightful lift.

How oblivious we are to the years
of agonizing struggles to perfect
what is casually watched from the tiers.
Only earnest attention can respect
how often the streams would dry if not for tears
to buoy the burden of graceful effect.

Garrett Buhl Robinson

Serenade
— for George Balanchine

Mr. B. sits at the tip of the wing,
he knows the piece, he knows what to expect,
there is always the inevitable misstep,
his interest now is watching the audience.
Behind the curtain, he knows the routine,
choice dancers of the corps, the trembling breath,
then the salve of the soothing release
and from this calm the strings begin to sing.
With an ethereal blue the curtain lifts
and the dancers — standing, enchanting,
after years reaching for the impossible —
touch the divine with their fingertips.
Then a whispered phrase as smooth as a pearl,
"Now, my dears, you may dance before the world."

Garrett Buhl Robinson

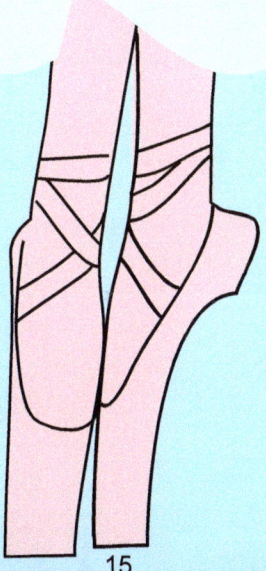

Mark Question

In regards to labels I draw a blank.
Just as most everyone else, I have been
called what others misthought of me
as well as what others had hoped would hurt,
but in countless times when I've made mistakes
what I've called myself has been the worst.
However, if you insist I will say
with the most confidence I can enlist,
having realized that my destination
is every moment in which I exist,
that all conclusions are inconclusive
and the only absolute I can give
is: if you feel you must label me
then label me a mystery.

Garrett Buhl Robinson

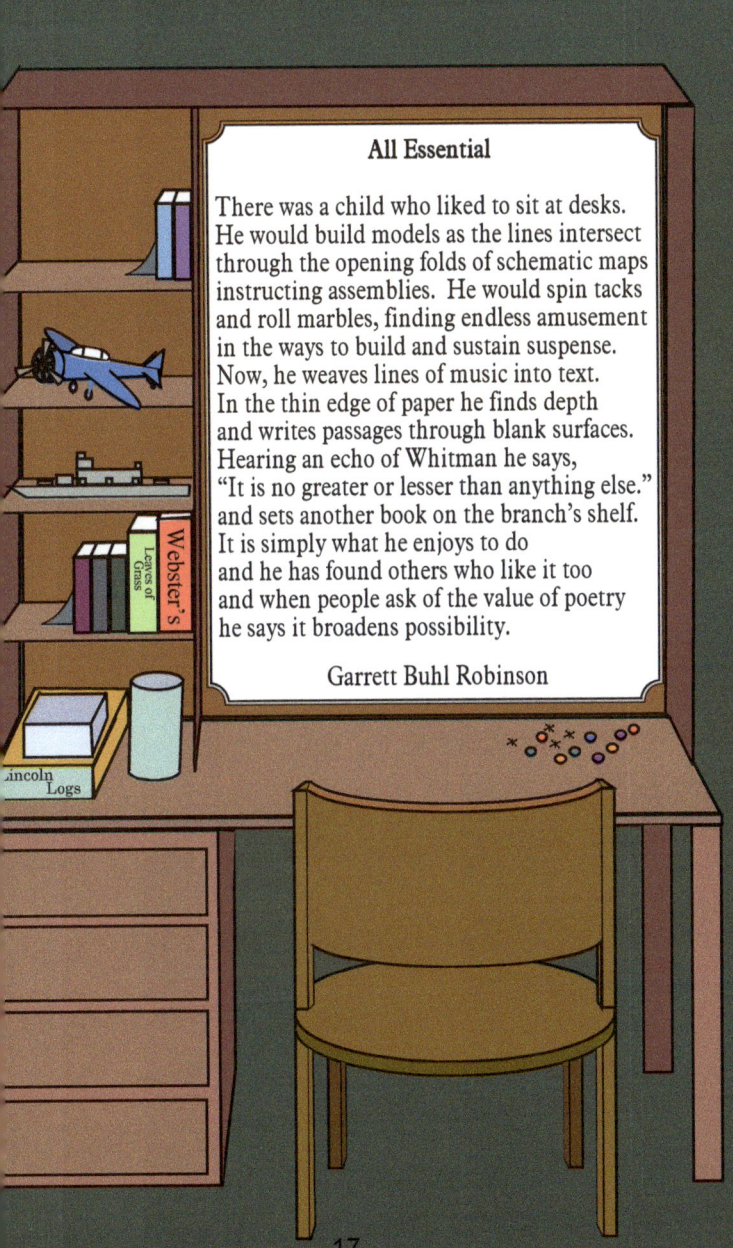

All Essential

There was a child who liked to sit at desks.
He would build models as the lines intersect
through the opening folds of schematic maps
instructing assemblies. He would spin tacks
and roll marbles, finding endless amusement
in the ways to build and sustain suspense.
Now, he weaves lines of music into text.
In the thin edge of paper he finds depth
and writes passages through blank surfaces.
Hearing an echo of Whitman he says,
"It is no greater or lesser than anything else."
and sets another book on the branch's shelf.
It is simply what he enjoys to do
and he has found others who like it too
and when people ask of the value of poetry
he says it broadens possibility.

Garrett Buhl Robinson

Creative Nature

The rural may be snubbed as raw and rude
except for the flourishing emergence
of talent from the outdoors' openness.
Call these the lines of a lyre or the flute's
capricious reeds, but the tones are tuned by life.
Wordsworth needed London just as Frost needed
New York. They romped into town in rustic weaves,
met in their publishers' lofty offices,
sang at gatherings, then ascended back
into the hills with evergreen limbs
growing to a close behind them
like a curtain of verdure on a worldly stage.
Talent is by nature original,
a living lecture of the ineffable.

        Garrett Buhl Robinson

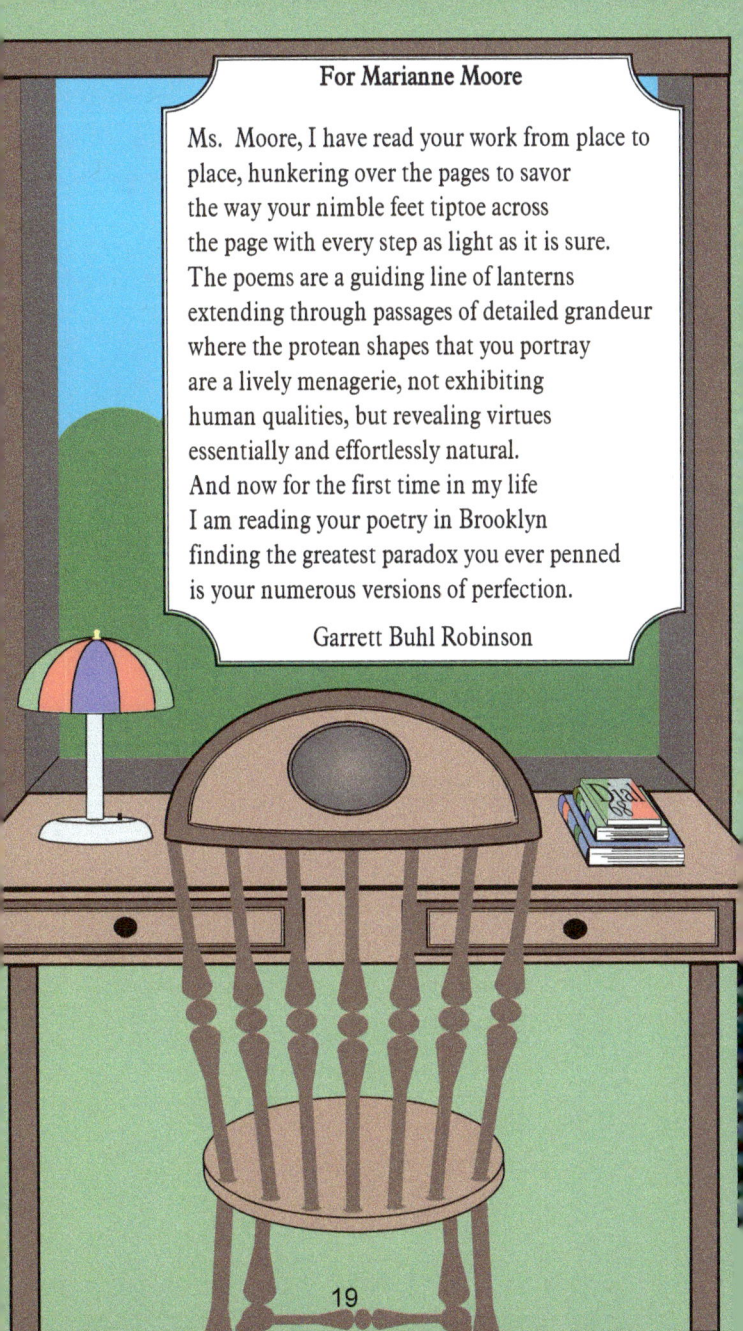

For Marianne Moore

Ms. Moore, I have read your work from place to
place, hunkering over the pages to savor
the way your nimble feet tiptoe across
the page with every step as light as it is sure.
The poems are a guiding line of lanterns
extending through passages of detailed grandeur
where the protean shapes that you portray
are a lively menagerie, not exhibiting
human qualities, but revealing virtues
essentially and effortlessly natural.
And now for the first time in my life
I am reading your poetry in Brooklyn
finding the greatest paradox you ever penned
is your numerous versions of perfection.

Garrett Buhl Robinson

Intimate with the Ancients

Through a solitary stretch sketched
upon a parchment surface,

hatched from the brooding memories
of isolation and interactions,

meticulously formulated
into ponderously balanced phrases

carried about clasped to the breast,
surviving rebuke and neglect,

announced from resounding mountains
and sipped with tender attention

through intimate statements
and broadening relations

while retaining rapturous meaning
through transcriptions and translations —

through the extending lengths of space and time
the reach of poets has touched my life.

Garrett Buhl Robinson

Hazel Hall

Many times I walked by her house.
The second floor in which she may
have stayed for several decades straight
was shroud in trees she'd never seen.
As bare as her view may have been,
no more than a gauzed glimpse outside
and taps on the glass to the birds in the sky,
she spun wonders purely of mind
in a chair she could never leave
until she softly slipped to sleep
after whorling skeins into arabesque dreams
now dancing through Portland in her poetry.

Garrett Buhl Robinson

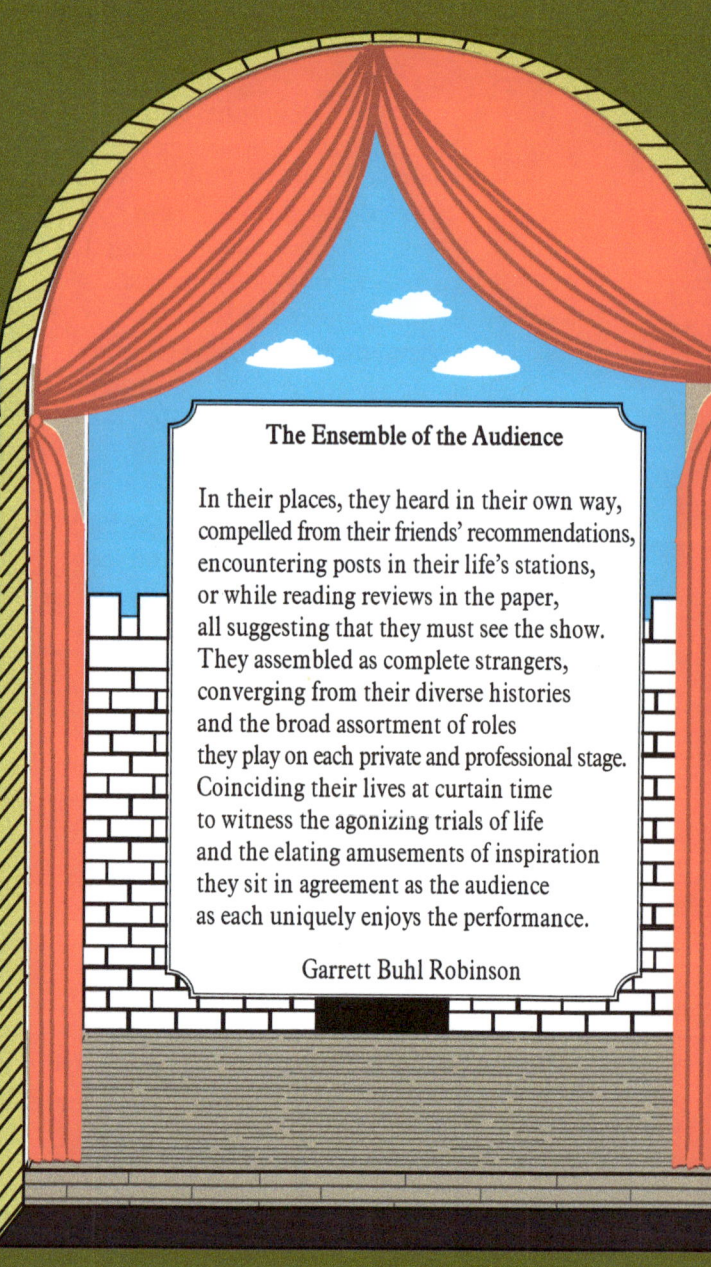

The Ensemble of the Audience

In their places, they heard in their own way,
compelled from their friends' recommendations,
encountering posts in their life's stations,
or while reading reviews in the paper,
all suggesting that they must see the show.
They assembled as complete strangers,
converging from their diverse histories
and the broad assortment of roles
they play on each private and professional stage.
Coinciding their lives at curtain time
to witness the agonizing trials of life
and the elating amusements of inspiration
they sit in agreement as the audience
as each uniquely enjoys the performance.

Garrett Buhl Robinson

Jester

Some work their whole lives to find the sublime
and scour the dark depths for a monstrous gift
but never realize the lightness and lift
in the pure sublimity of a smile.

Some compile dense mountains for their pulpit
but the most astounding profundity
resounds through expansive simplicity
confessed with the blessings of openness.

Some say pleasure is found where they reside,
fulfilling themselves in what they obtain,
but the greatest gain I could ever claim
has always been found in all that I give.

My grandiloquence is a shrewd gesture —
pleasing others is my greatest pleasure.

Garrett Buhl Robinson

For Ms. Bee

I am terribly sorry little bee.
I certainly did not intend to tease
but the open flowers on the sleeves
of my books displayed so alluringly
are only the prints of photography.

While you buzz back and forth busily
I humbly offer an apology
because I know the nectar that you seek
is not the type of nectar on these leaves —
they are written to be read, not to eat.

With all your eyes I'm surprised you can't see
but you see a different world than me
and while I write sweet figures in poetry
you make your honey literally.

                Garrett Buhl Robinson

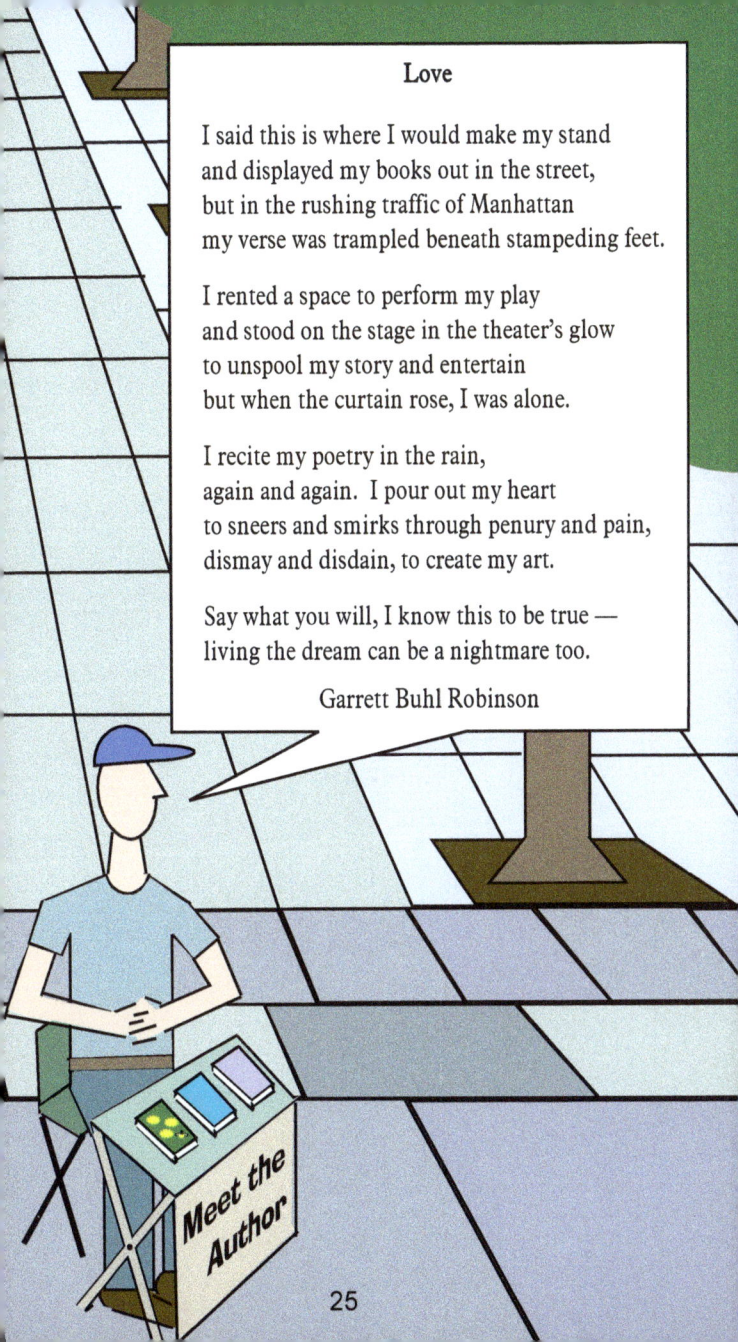

Love

I said this is where I would make my stand
and displayed my books out in the street,
but in the rushing traffic of Manhattan
my verse was trampled beneath stampeding feet.

I rented a space to perform my play
and stood on the stage in the theater's glow
to unspool my story and entertain
but when the curtain rose, I was alone.

I recite my poetry in the rain,
again and again. I pour out my heart
to sneers and smirks through penury and pain,
dismay and disdain, to create my art.

Say what you will, I know this to be true —
living the dream can be a nightmare too.

Garrett Buhl Robinson

Maps Are Metaphors

I have often thought of topography
to map the rough terrain of my life
where tight increments of lines steeply climb
and swiftly slide through creases of ravines
washing with the watersheds as they spread
in fanning planes that slip beneath the sloughs
of a glass lake where the soft plop
from a raindrop sends ripples on the body
of water's settled, reflective repose
so the whole sky begins to wave overhead.

Or perhaps these rings of lyrics outline
a mountain, tightening as they rise,
narrowing to one peak from every side
ascending to touch the attentive mind.

            Garrett Buhl Robinson

Proof of Life

Some have said the lines of a sonnet are
the bars of a jail but this is simply
a matter of perspective. What I see
are the strings of an elegant harp.
I see rays of warmth leaping from the sun.
I see a flight of stairs that softly rise
to an open door for a dreamy night.
I see ripples of a river as it runs
from the headwaters of the Renaissance,
gathering in trickling rivulets
splashing laughter and meandering music.
I see the soft ribs of a celestial
being with a heart moving fluid life
and lungs swelling with the air that inspires.

Garrett Buhl Robinson

Made of Strays

Stumbling through the woods on a moonless night
among the fronds of ferns and mossy stone
I found a plume fallen long ago,
the only trace of a trackless flight.
Then with some twigs from the forest floor
still wet and green from early Spring
and an unraveled quilt's colorful string
I wove a nest I left above the hayloft's door.
Although empty when I turned away
I hoped some saddened thought would settle there
and find comfort from the frosty air
cupped inside the tender weave of strays,
then with the next day's warming light
dive into the bottomless sea of sky.

Garrett Buhl Robinson

Troubadour

Love? Could anyone bear another poem
about love? Why would someone want to read
as a substitute for reality?
Or is it just a manifestation
of adoration's treacherous deception?
Aren't we always disappointed to see
what our desires had imagined to be?
Perhaps it is best to leave love alone
rather than spoil what we had hoped would come.
Yet, poems are all that love is to me
so I put all my love into poetry
and make sweet love with others through my songs.
I may cry inside for my entire life
but I'll blossom and bloom for other's eyes.

Garrett Buhl Robinson

For a Romantic

There are some who believe poems are writ
from the themes and theories we invent
as if inspiration was the conscript
of a very specific determinant
that was made with formulas and instruments
so that the unexpected was from intent
and surprise was merely mismanagement
from a factory of ambiguousness.

Then reading your verse earlier today,
listening to the words and all they say,
I began to float on the music they made
from the melodies in every phrase
along the correspondence you arranged
with the chords inlaid and delicately played
and carried by a cadence sustained
by the beat of your heart upon the page.

Poems are not contrived from designs,
they are released from within, deep inside,
and the deeper one's concentration dives
the higher one's inspiration flies,
making brazen leaps to span the divides
in the endless potential of our lives
from the wonder of a child's awakening mind
to the timeless kindness in a grandmother's eyes.

Garrett Buhl Robinson

Photo © Bob Kidd
bobkiddphotography.com

Garrett Buhl Robinson is a poet living in New York City.

If you enjoyed this book, you can order other titles from your favorite bookstore or request them at your local library.

Some other titles by Garrett Buhl Robinson:

<u>Poetry</u>
City of Poems
The Ballad of Emperor Norton
The Nobody
Always Here Always Odd
Beauty beyond Reason
Martha, a poem

<u>Fiction</u>
Zoë
Nunatak

Poet in the Park™

In Humanity I see Grace, Beauty and Dignity.

PoetinthePark.com

www.ingramcontent.com/pod-product-compliance
Lightning Source LLC
Chambersburg PA
CBHW061732070526
44583CB00024B/3107